SCHOLASTIC

GRADES K–1

Sequencing Practice Mini-Books

By Maria Fleming

New York · Toronto · London · Auckland · Sydney
Mexico City · New Delhi · Hong Kong · Buenos Aires

Teaching *Resources*

Edited by Immacula A. Rhodes
Cover design by Jason Robinson
Cover illustrations by Bari Weissman
Interior design by Sydney Wright
Illustrations by Anne Kennedy and Bari Weissman

ISBN-13: 978-0-545-24802-0
ISBN-10: 0-545-24802-7

3 4 5 6 7 8 9 10   40   17 16 15 14 13 12

Contents

Introduction

Welcome to *Sequencing Practice Mini-Books: Grades K–1!* The 25 mini-books in this resource are designed to improve children's reading comprehension by focusing on a key skill: sequencing. As children make each mini-book, they will identify the sequence of events and put the pages in time order. Recognizing that stories have a beginning, a middle, and an end and that events happen in a logical order provides students with a framework for understanding what they read.

Organized by season, these easy-to-make mini-books include fiction and nonfiction selections that help children celebrate seasonal changes, mark special occasions, and explore favorite themes, such as apples, pumpkins, penguins, valentines, plants, butterflies, sunny-day fun, and more. The variety of formats challenges children to examine picture and/or text clues—including important time-order vocabulary, such as *first, next, then, before, after, last,* and *finally*—to sequence the pages for assembly. The mini-books in each group increase in difficulty to provide maximum flexibility, allowing you to meet the needs of children at different ability levels as well as to create a progression of sequencing activities that reflect their growing comprehension skills. You can use the mini-books for whole-class or partner activities or in small groups. The books also work well as learning-center or take-home activities.

Finally, and perhaps most important, the mini-books are designed to reinforce the idea that reading is both useful and fun. As children create the books, they discover that reading can help them perform a task; learn about a person, animal, activity, or subject that interests them; or simply provide pleasure as they follow the adventures of an engaging character.

Why Sequencing Is Important

Recognizing sequence plays an important role in children's reading comprehension. "Readers can discover a sequence in connected illustrations: chronological order, cycles of action from home to an adventure and back home, flashbacks, embedded stories. Attention to the illustrations can support understanding of text structure (thinking about the text)" (Fountas & Pinnell, 2006). Whether in pictures or text, early exposure to sequencing opens the gateway to thinking critically, helping children apply prior knowledge to understand unfamiliar texts, storylines, and procedures.

As children progress from pre-reading to becoming proficient readers, sequencing stories fosters the development of other skills within Bloom's Taxonomy, helping children to predict, summarize, explain, and discuss story events. Understanding how events play out—in stories and real life—aids readers in anticipating what comes next and in recognizing what is expected, reasonable, and logical. When this occurs, comprehension deepens.

To progress in reading, readers must also understand the most basic nature of the story itself. "*Knowledge of narrative structure* involves understanding the nature of stories and how they are constructed. Knowledge of the structure of stories is important because most of the material used to teach reading to young children is written in narrative form. Children are likely to understand material presented in a form with which they are familiar" (Strickland, 1998). Understanding sequence helps children better understand the structure of a story and aids them in recalling and recounting important events in an organized, logical way.

Resources

Fountas, Irene C. and Gay Su Pinnell, 2006. *Teaching for comprehending and fluency: Thinking, talking, and writing about reading, K–8.* Portsmouth, NH: Heinemann.

Strickland, Dorothy S., 1998. *Teaching phonics today: A primer for educators.* Newark, DE: International Reading Association.

How to Make the Mini-Books

Copy the reproducible patterns for each mini-book, including text boxes where applicable. Distribute the patterns to children and have them assemble their mini-books according to the type of mini-book they'll be constructing (see below). After they correctly order and number the pages, help children stack and staple the pages together behind the cover. (If needed, use the Answer Key on pages 76-80 to check the page sequence before binding the mini-book.)

Three-Page Mini-Books

Children "read" the pictures to sequence the pages of these mini-books.

1. After distributing the pages, point out that they have pictures only on them.
2. Offer guidance as children study the pictures to look for clues that will help them sequence the pages.
3. After they correctly order the pages, tell children to fill in the page numbers.

Lots of Leaves (page 9)
The Spooky Spider (page 11)
Time to Brush! (page 25)
How to Make a Snowman
   (page 27)
Growing a Garden (page 41)
Puddle Problem (page 43)
A Treat to Share (page 60)
Cool in the Pool (page 62)

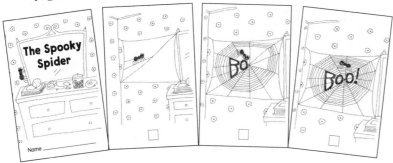

Four-Page Mini-Books

Children match a text box to the picture on each page and then sequence the pages of these mini-books.

1. After distributing the pages, have children cut out the four text boxes.
2. Point out that each page of the book has a picture as well as an empty box under the picture. Explain that children will read the text boxes and then use picture clues to match each text box to its corresponding picture. Once they've matched the correct text to each page, have children glue the text boxes to the pages.
3. Tell children to use picture and text clues to put the pages in order. After they correctly order the pages, have them fill in the page numbers.

Gus the Bus (page 13)
A Gift for Bear (page 29)
Becoming a Frog (page 45)
The Life of a Butterfly
   (page 48)
Hermit Crab's New House
   (page 64)

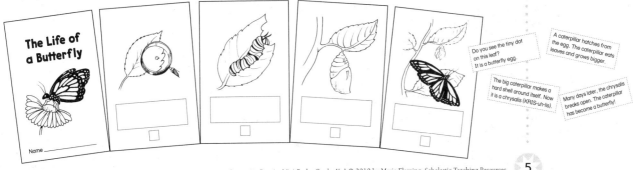

Before You Start

The mini-book pages are sequenced in the correct order in this resource. To distribute the pages in random order, copy a class supply of the mini-book pages and use a paper cutter to cut the pages apart. You can then stack the pages for each mini-book in random order before distributing them to children.

Five-Page Mini-Books
Illustrations and Text

These mini-books have words and pictures on every page. Children use both textual and visual clues to sequence the pages.

1. After distributing the pages to children, point out that the pages have both pictures and text.

2. Offer guidance as children look for clues in the illustrations and text that will help them sequence the pages.

3. After children correctly order the pages, have them fill in the page numbers.

Text Only

These mini-books include only text on the pages, allowing children to provide their own illustration for each page.

1. After distributing the pages, point out that they contain text, but no pictures.

2. Have children read each page, looking for clues in the text to help them sequence the pages. Offer guidance as needed.

3. After children correctly order the pages, have them draw a picture to match the text on each page and then fill in the page number. Also, have them illustrate the cover. Before they do, talk about how the illustration and title on a book's cover usually relate to the main idea of the story and help readers know what the book is about.

Extension Activities

Use these additional ideas to help reinforce sequencing skills.

Sandwich Sequence: Introduce the mini-books with a simple demonstration and discussion about sequencing. Bring in sandwich-making materials and ask children to watch closely as you assemble a sandwich. Afterward, invite volunteers to describe the process. Offer prompts such as, "What did I do first? What did I do next? What was the last step?" Then write the steps of the process on sentence strips and place them in order in a pocket chart. Read the sentences aloud. Explain to children that putting things in time order is called sequencing. Ask them to tell why it is important to know the order in which things happen. Then mix up the sentence strips in the pocket chart and read them aloud again. Ask: *Are these directions for making the sandwich clear or confusing? If you tried to make the sandwich in this order, what problems might you have?* Conclude by having children put the sentences back in their proper sequence.

Favorite Stories: Photocopy several scenes from a picture book that children know well. (Mask any accompanying text.) Choose one or two scenes from the beginning, middle, and end of the book. Glue each picture to a separate sheet of tagboard. Then line the pictures up in random order. Explain to children that events in a story happen in a certain order. This is called the story sequence, and it helps readers understand what they read. Then have children work together to sequence the pictures. Talk about how clues in the pictures can help them figure out the proper order. Finally, invite volunteers to use the picture sequence to retell the story.

Signal Words: Help familiarize students with key vocabulary that can signal time order. To begin, write these signal words on chart paper: *first, next, then, before, after, last, finally.* Do students notice anything special about these words? What do they have in common? Explain that all of the words give hints about when something happens. They can be very helpful in telling the time order—or sequence—of events that happen in a story. Then ask children to look and listen for these words and others that might signal time order on their mini-book pages. (They might circle or highlight the words.) Encourage them to use the signal words as clues in sequencing their pages.

Pocket Charts: Any of the mini-books can easily be adapted to a pocket chart activity. Simply write the mini-book text on sentence strips or use the illustrations to create picture cards. (Or make cards with both the text and illustrations.) Place the sentence strips or picture cards out of sequence in a pocket chart. Then invite children to put them in the proper order. As they work, encourage children to talk about the picture or text clues that help them make their decisions about the story sequence.

Graphic Organizers: Students can demonstrate their understanding of story sequence with graphic organizers. To create a basic graphic organizer, draw a ladder on chart paper. Then choose a mini-book and invite volunteers to tell about each main event in the story sequence. Write their responses on the ladder rungs, starting with the first event on the bottom and moving to the top. To help guide children, you might ask questions such as, "What happens first in the story? What happens next? Then what happens? What happens after that? What happens last?" For variety, you can create graphic organizers that reflect the theme of a particular mini-book. For example, for "How to Make a Snowman" (page 27), you might draw a simple snowman and label the snowballs "First," "Next," and "Last." Similarly, you might draw a gift box for "A Gift for Bear" (page 29), including a ribbon that divides the box into four quadrants to be labeled "First," "Next," "Then," and "Last."

More Mini-Books: Invite children to make their own sequencing mini-books. Suggest that they choose a familiar activity as the basis of their story. For example, they might create a book about how they get ready for school, how to make a snow angel, how to fly a kite, or how to give a dog a bath. Children can write or dictate the text for each page of their book. As they work with their story, encourage them to use sequencing signal words such as *first, next, then, before, after, last,* and *finally*. Have children illustrate their pages and then bind them behind a cover. If desired, ask children to omit the page numbers. Then punch holes in the pages and tie them together with yarn or string so that children can take their books apart and challenge others to sequence the pages.

Connections to the Language Arts Standards

Mid-continent Research for Education and Learning (McREL), a nationally recognized nonprofit organization, has compiled and evaluated national and state standards—and proposed what teachers should provide for their K–1 students to grow proficient in reading. The activities in this book support the following standards:

Uses the general skills and strategies of the reading process including:
- Uses mental images and meaning clues based on pictures and print to aid in comprehension of text
- Uses basic elements of phonetic and structural analysis to decode unknown words
- Understands level-appropriate sight words and vocabulary
- Uses self-correction strategies

Uses reading skills and strategies to understand and interpret a variety of literary texts including:
- Knows the sequence of events in a story
- Understands a variety of literary passages and texts
- Knows setting, main characters, main events, sequence, and problems in stories

Uses reading skills and strategies to understand and interpret a variety of informational texts including:
- Understands a variety of informational texts
- Understands the main idea and supporting details of simple expository information
- Summarizes information found in texts (retells in own words)
- Relates new information to prior knowledge and experience

Source: Kendall, J. S., & Marzano, R. J. (2004). *Content knowledge: A compendium of standards and benchmarks for K–12 education.* Aurora, CO: Mid-continent Research for Education and Learning. Online database: **http://www.mcrel.org/standards-benchmarks/**

Lots of
Leaves

Name _____

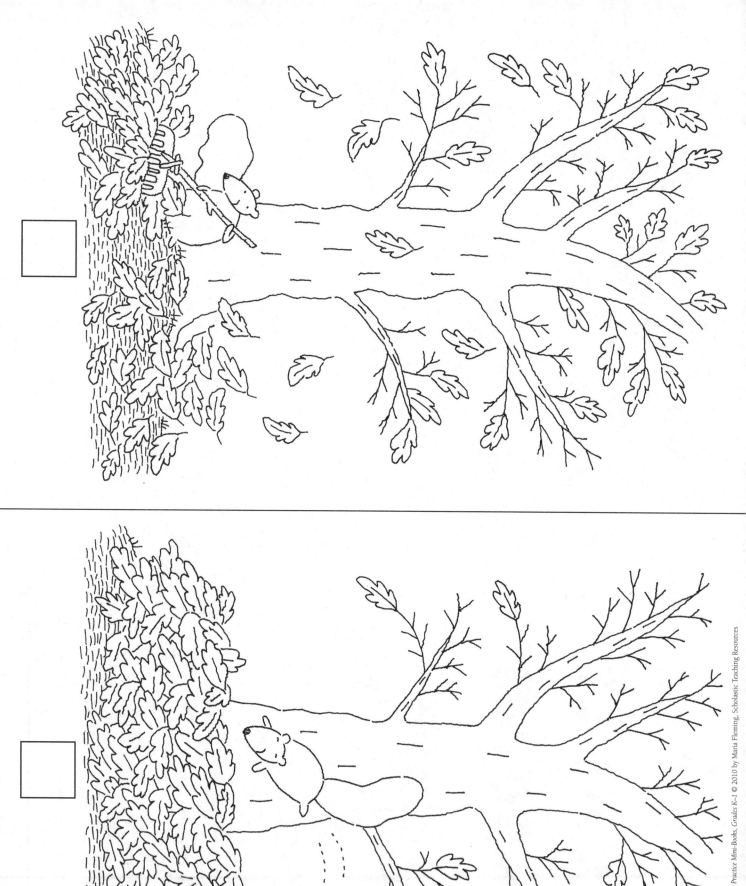

The Spooky Spider

Name _____

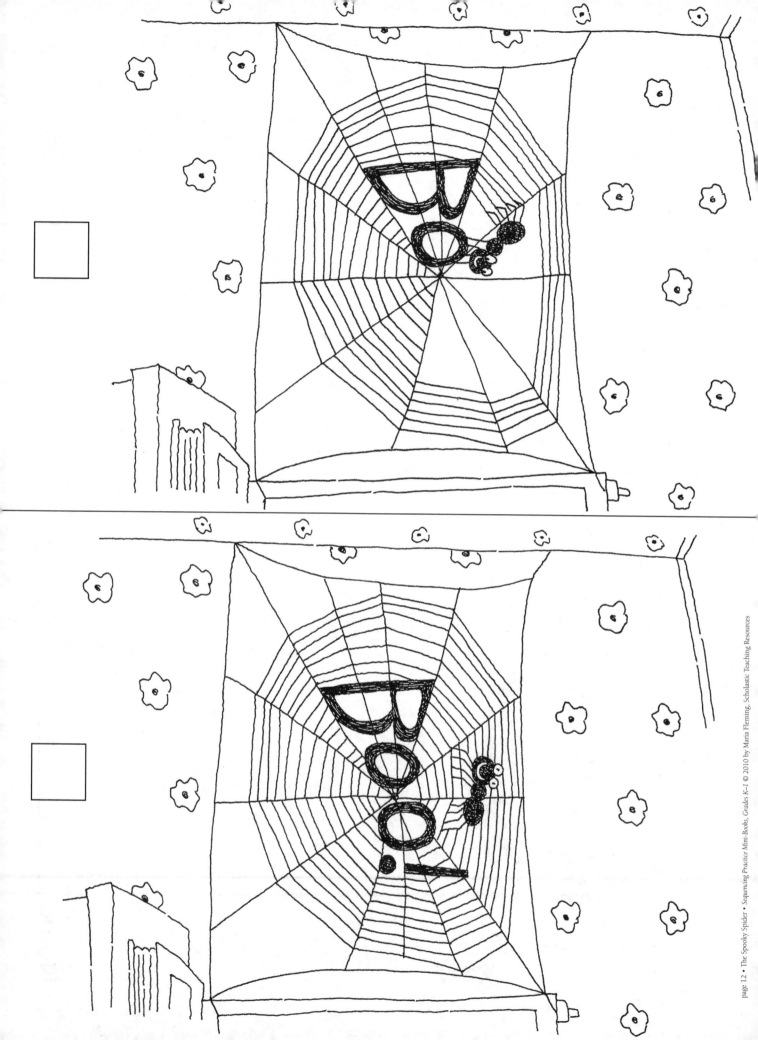

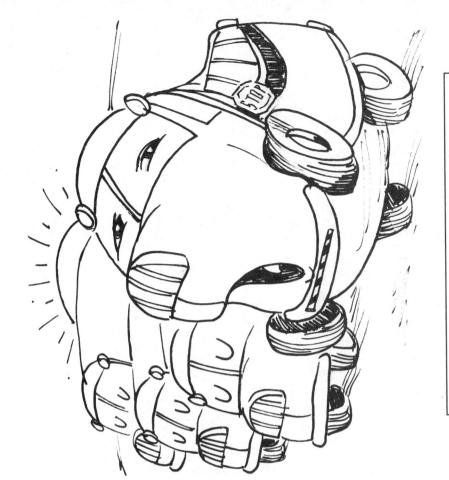

Glue text box here.

Gus the Bus

Name _____

Glue text box here.

Glue text box here.

Gus the bus wakes
with the sun.
There's work to do.
No time for fun.

The driver says,
"Good morning, Gus!"
She climbs on board
and starts the bus.

Gus makes stops
on many streets.
Sleepy children
fill his seats.

At school, the children
all get out.
"Hooray for Gus the bus!"
they shout.

Glue text box here.

Apple Pie Day

Name _____

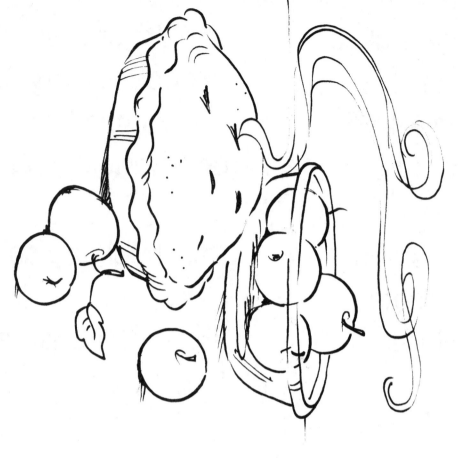

Let's go pick some apples.
Fill the basket high.
Let's bring the apples home
and make an apple pie.

Next, we mix the apples
with sugar and some spices.

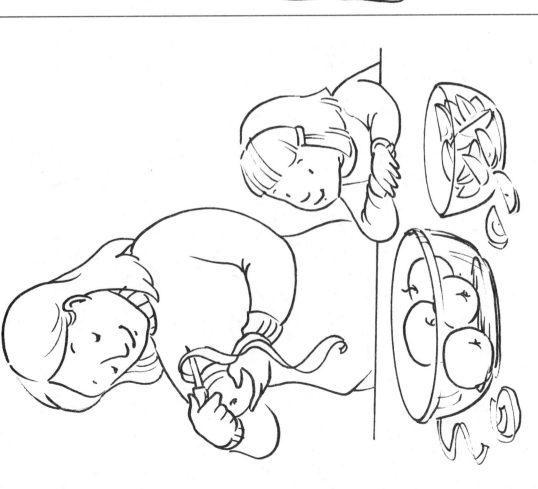

First, we peel the apples.
We cut them into slices.

We put the apples in a crust.
Then it's time to bake it.

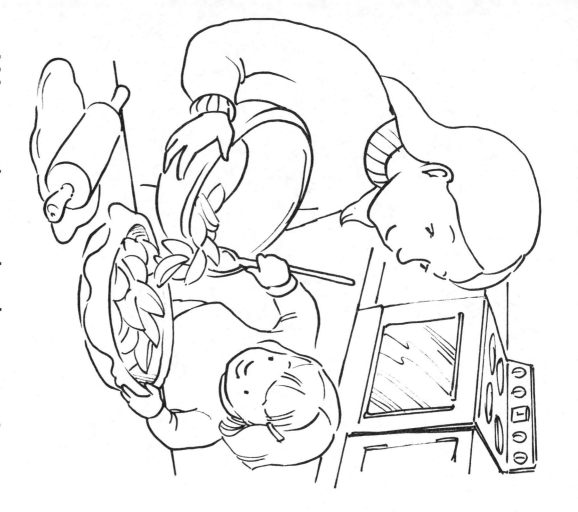

Look! Our apple pie is done.
It was fun to make it!

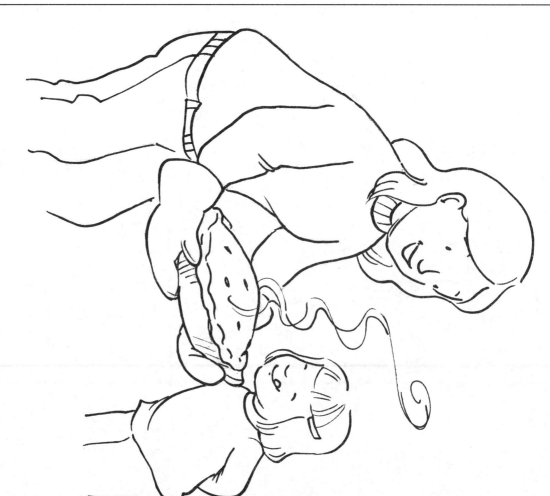

I'm going to make
a jack-o'-lantern!
Here is my pumpkin.

My
Jack-O'-Lantern

Name _____

First, I make the eyes.

Next, I make a nose.

Finally, I add a silly hat.
Now I'm done!

After the nose, I make a mouth.

Let's Make
Turkey Treats

Name _____

Let's make a special turkey craft together. First, fold a piece of paper into a fan.

☐

Then draw the turkey's face and wings. Cut them out.

Next, glue the fan onto a paper cup. These are the turkey's feathers.

Now glue the face and wings onto the cup. Then fill the cup with a yummy treat.

Finally, it's time to gobble, gobble up your treat!

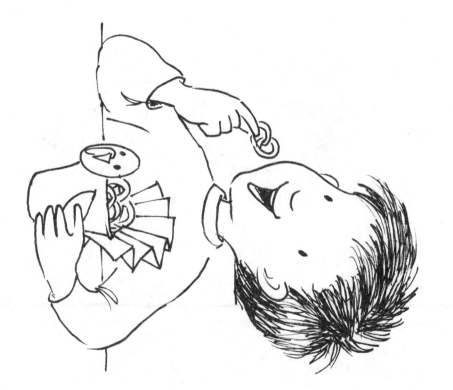

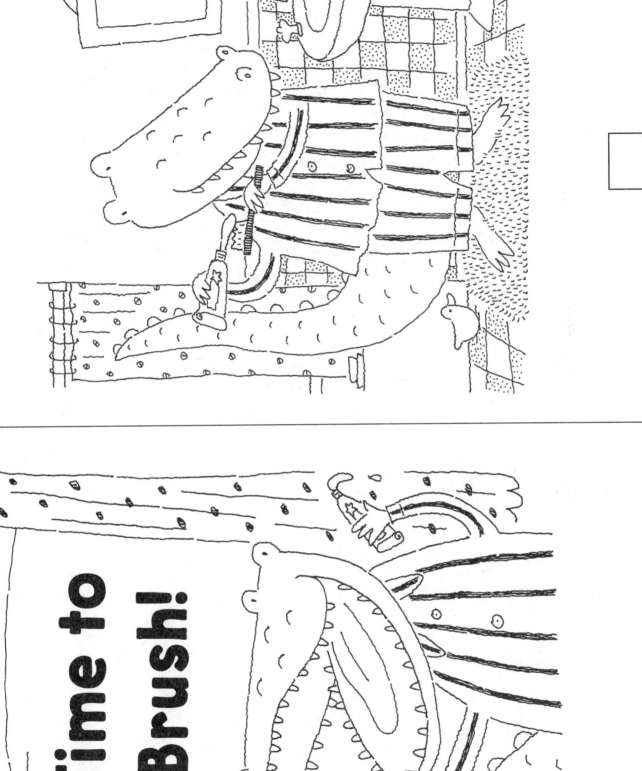

Time to Brush!

Name _____

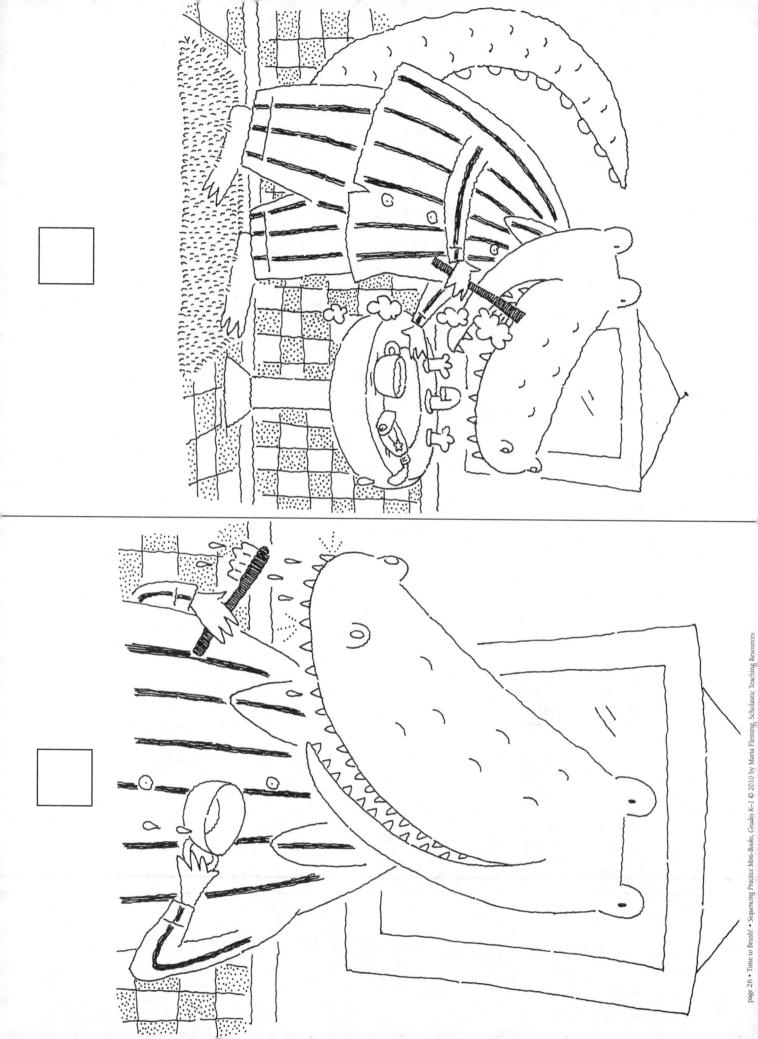

How to Make a Snowman

Name _____

Glue text box here.

A Gift for Bear

Name _____

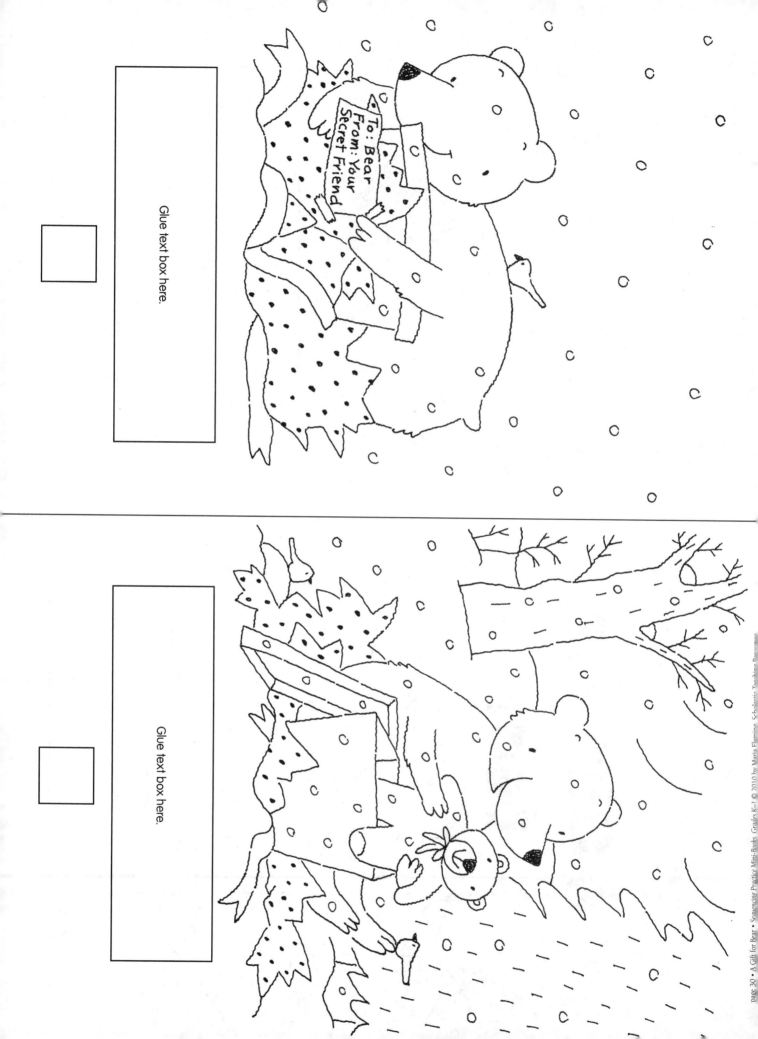

Glue text box here.

To: Bear
From: Your
Secret Friend

Glue text box here.

Winter will not
seem so cold
with a teddy bear
to hold.

It's a teddy bear for you!

Look over there,
under that tree.
It's a gift!
What can it be?

Take off the bow
and paper, too.

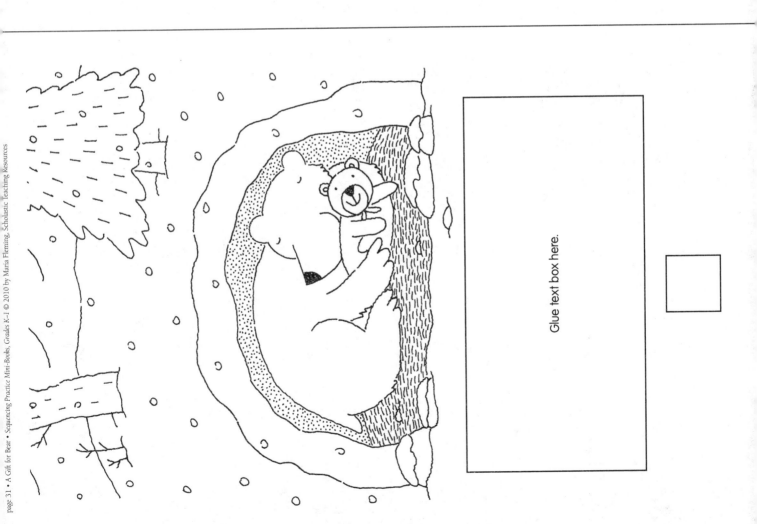

Glue text box here.

Groundhog's Winter

Name _____

Before winter comes,
groundhog eats lots of plants.
He will not eat all winter long.

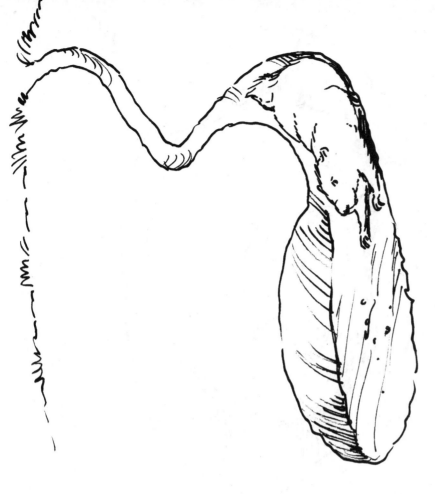

Groundhog digs a long tunnel
with a small room at the end.
This is called a burrow.

Now groundhog is nice and fat.
He begins to dig a hole.

Groundhog sleeps in his burrow
all winter. This long, deep sleep
is called hibernation.

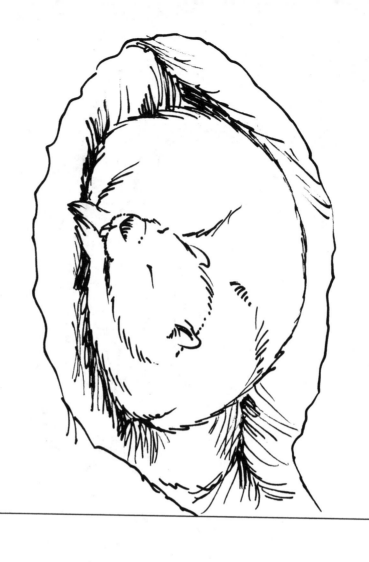

At last, winter is over.
Groundhog leaves his burrow
to stretch out in the warm sun.

Peck, peck, peck!
A penguin chick hatches
from an egg.

A Penguin Grows Up

Name _____

After it hatches, the chick is hungry. The penguin parents feed it.

The chick eats and eats. It grows fast. Now it has fluffy gray feathers.

At last, the penguin is all grown up! It dives into the sea with the other penguins.

Then the chick loses its gray fluff. It grows black and white feathers like its parents.

A Valentine for Max

Name _____

This is my cat, Max. I want to make him a valentine.

Next, I write his name
inside the heart.

First, I draw a big heart.

Then I draw small hearts around his name.

☐

Finally, I give Max the valentine. Max loves it! And I love Max.

☐

Growing a Garden

Name _____

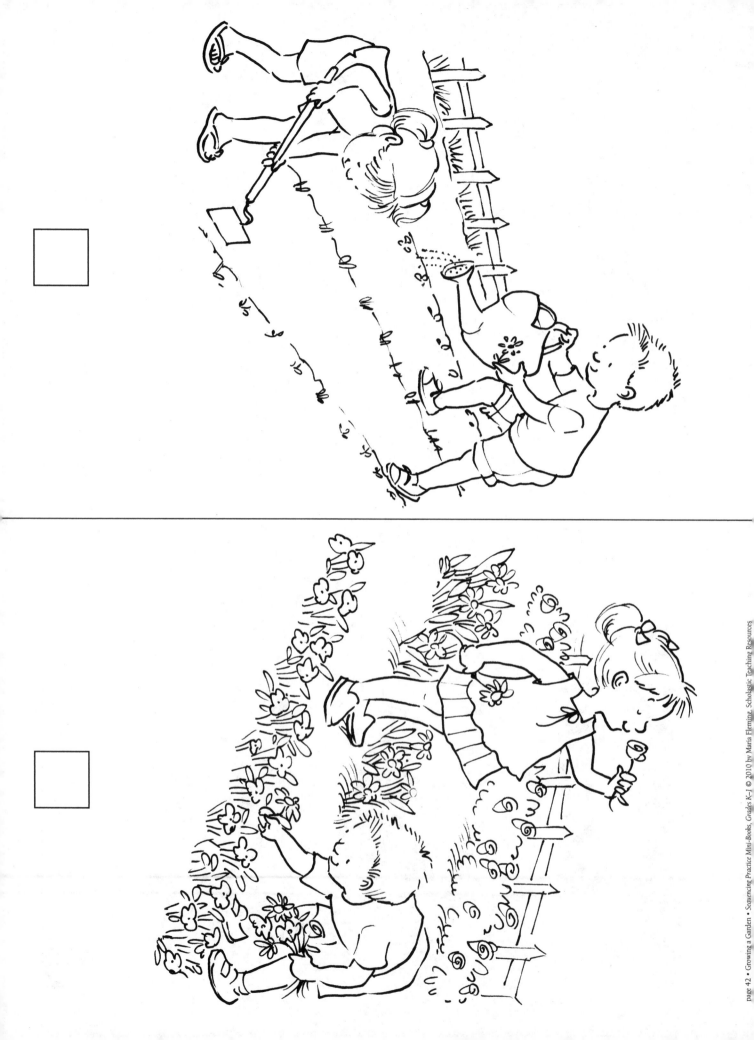

Puddle
Problem

Name _____

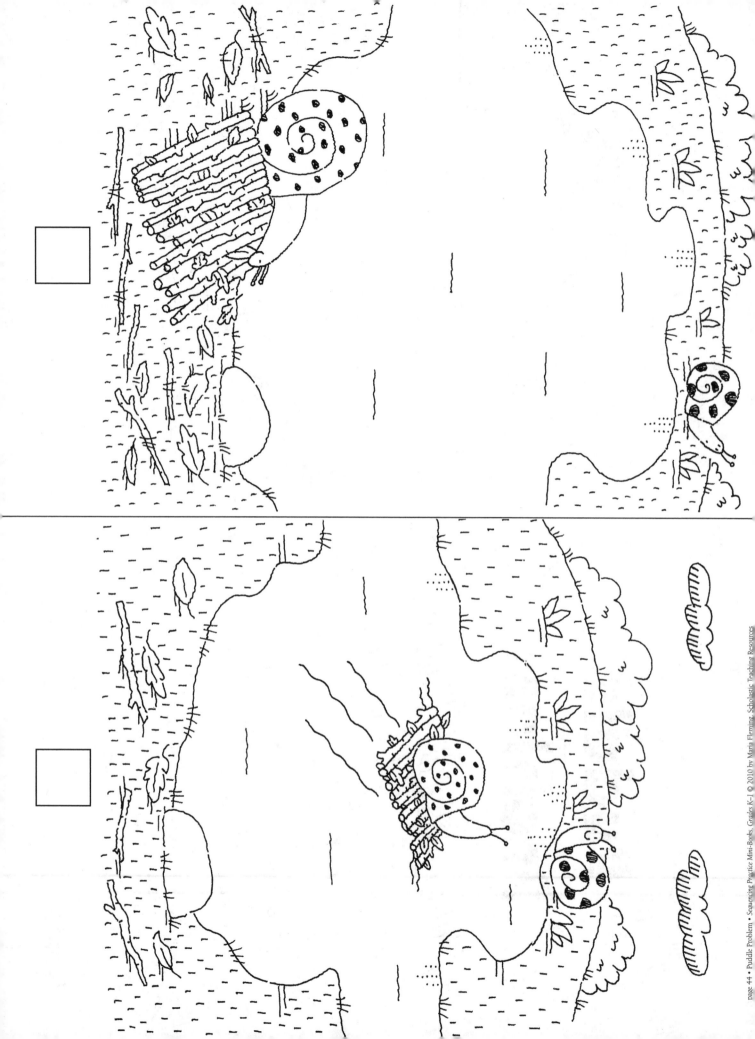

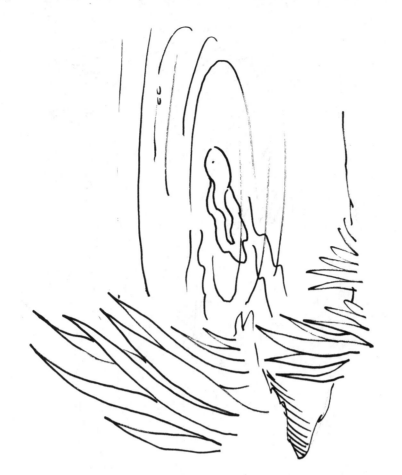

Glue text box here.

Becoming
a Frog

Name _____

Glue text box here.

Glue text box here.

Next, the tadpole's eyes and mouth grow bigger. Its tail is almost gone now.

First, the tadpole grows legs. Its tail gets shorter.

At last, the tadpole has become a frog! It leaves the water to live on land.

This little tadpole is about to go through big changes.

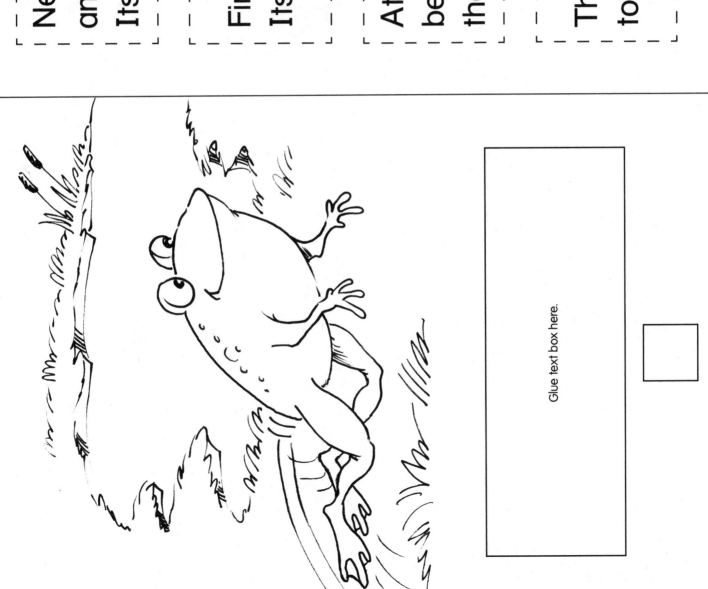

Glue text box here.

Sequencing Practice Mini-Books, Grades K–1 © 2010 by Maria Fleming, Scholastic Teaching Resources

Name _____

The Life of a Butterfly

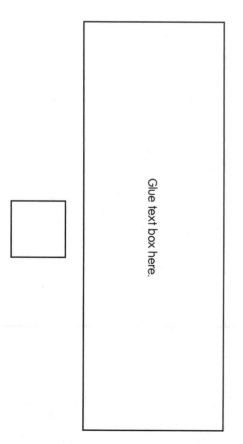

Glue text box here.

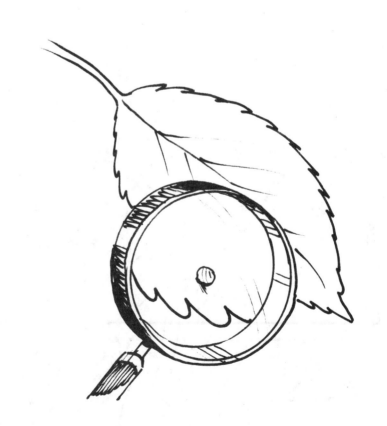

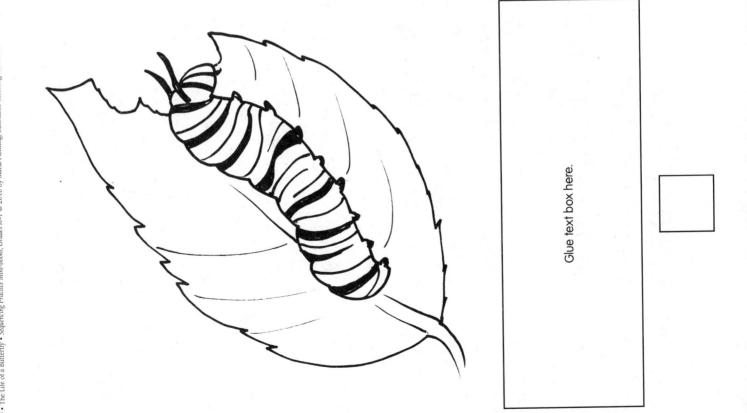

Glue text box here.

Glue text box here.

Glue text box here.

A caterpillar hatches from the egg. The caterpillar eats leaves and grows bigger.

Do you see the tiny dot on this leaf? It is a butterfly egg.

Many days later, the chrysalis breaks open. The caterpillar has become a butterfly!

The big caterpillar makes a hard shell around itself. Now it is a chrysalis (KRIS-uh-lis).

Whee!
I can fly!

Five little raindrops
fell from the sky.
The first one said,
"Whee! I can fly!"

Five Little
Raindrops

Name _____

The second one said,
"Ready, set, go!"

The third one said,
"Look out below!"

The fifth one said,
"Here comes the sun!"
And that was the end
of the raindrops' fun.

The fourth one said,
"Wait for me, everyone!"

Get Ready for
Baby Birds

Name _____

Baby birds will be here soon!
First, mama bird makes a nest.

Soon baby birds hatch from
the eggs. Hello, little chicks!

Then she lays eggs in the nest.

Next, mama bird feeds
the chicks worms.

At last, the chicks
are big! They fly away.
Bye, mama bird!

Sheep came first with big balloons.

The Surprise Party

Name _____

Pig came second with ice cream and spoons.

Hen came third with hats to wear.

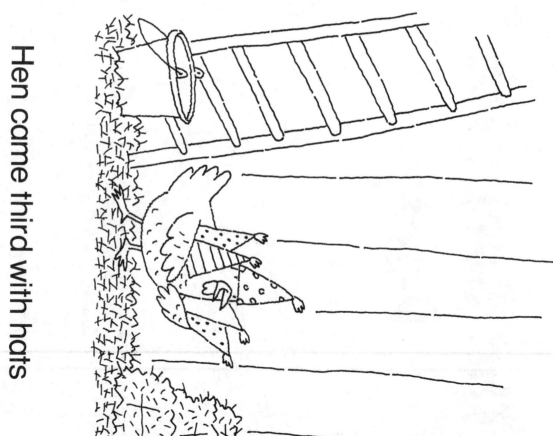

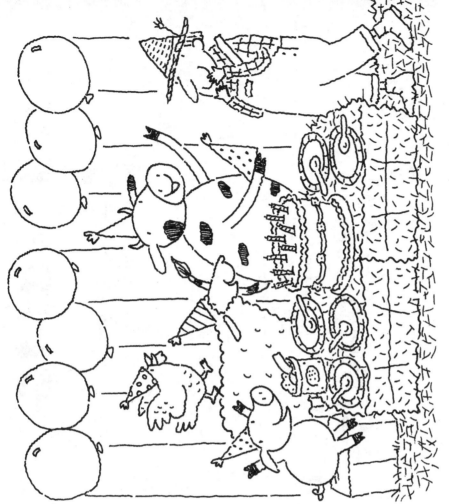

Who came last? Farmer Fred!

"HAPPY BIRTHDAY!"

everybody said.

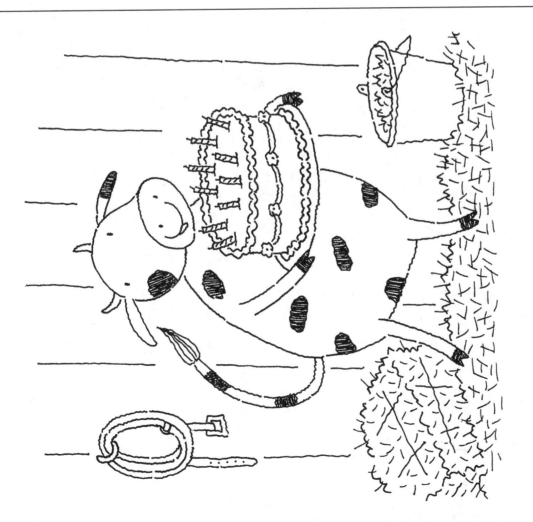

Cow came fourth with cake

to share.

Name _____

A Treat to Share

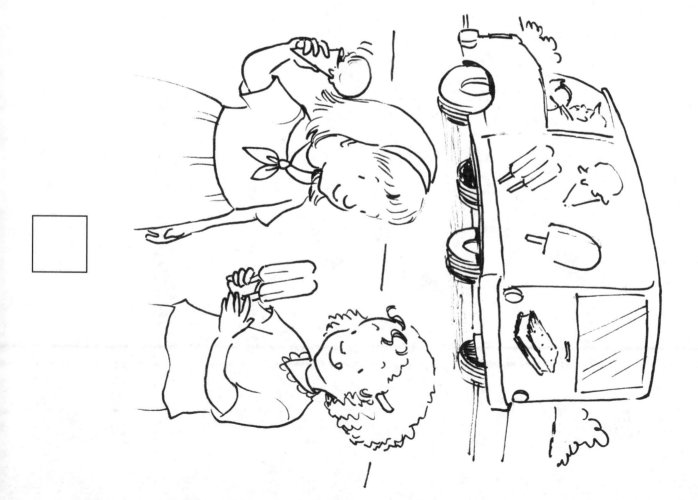

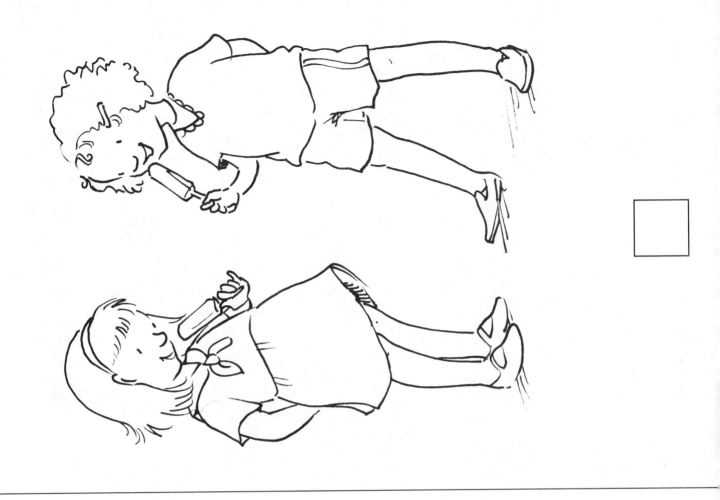

Name _____

Cool in the Pool

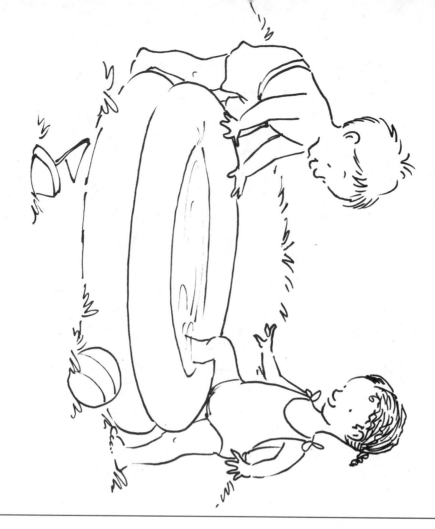

Hermit Crab's New House

Name _____

Glue text box here.

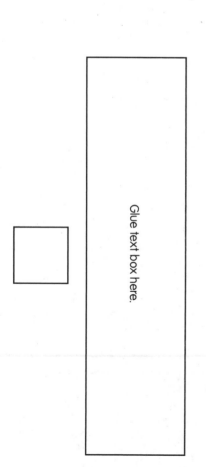

Glue text box here.

Glue text box here.

Glue text box here.

Oh, well. My new home is gone. I will put my shell back on.

This sandcastle looks just right!

I need a new house. My shell is too tight.

Oh no! Here comes a wave! It's very big! I must be brave!

Please come play with me.

Ladybug called her best friend, Bee. She said, "Please come play with me."

Ladybug and Bee

Name _____

First, they hid
among the flowers.

Next, they rode
their bikes for hours.

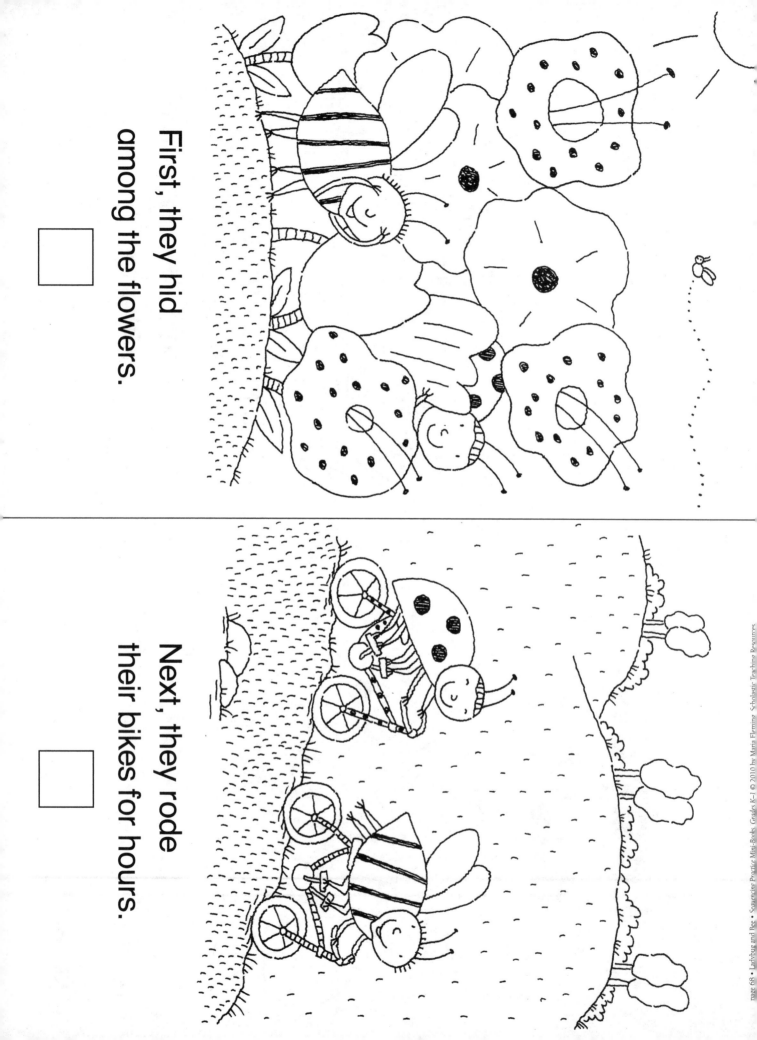

They said goodbye
when it got dark.

Last, they see-sawed
in the park.

Name _____

The Great
Big Carrot

One day, rabbit found
a great big carrot.
She pulled its leafy top.

"Let me help," said mouse.

Mouse pulled turtle.

Turtle pulled rabbit.

Rabbit pulled the carrot.

But the carrot would not

come up.

"Let me help," said turtle.

Turtle pulled rabbit.

Rabbit pulled the carrot.

But the carrot would not

come up.

"Let me help," said
an itty-bitty bug.
She grabbed mouse's tail.
Then the itty-bitty bug
gave a great big tug.

POP! Up came the carrot!
Then they all had
a delicious carrot feast.
And the itty-bitty bug
ate the biggest piece!

It's picnic time! What's inside
our picnic basket?

Our Picnic
Lunch

Name _____

First, we take out sandwiches.

Next, we take out apples.

Finally, we take out cookies. What a yummy lunch to munch!

After the apples, we take out grapes.

Answer Key

Lots of Leaves (pages 9–10)

Lots of Leaves

Name _____

1

2

3

The Spooky Spider (pages 11–12)

The Spooky Spider

Name _____

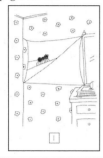

1

2

3

Gus the Bus (pages 13–15)

Gus the Bus

Name _____

Gus the bus wakes with the sun. There's work to do. No time for fun.

1

The driver says, "Good morning, Gus!" She climbs on board and starts the bus.

2

Gus makes stops on many streets. Sleepy children fill his seats.

3

At school, the children all get out. "Hooray for Gus the bus!" they shout.

4

Apple Pie Day (pages 16–18)

Apple Pie Day

Name _____

Let's go pick some apples. Fill the basket high. Let's bring the apples home and make an apple pie.

1

First, we peel the apples. We cut them into slices.

2

Next, we mix the apples with sugar and some spices.

3

We put the apples in a crust. Then it's time to bake it.

4

Look! Our apple pie is done. It was fun to make it!

5

My Jack-O'-Lantern (pages 19–21)

My Jack-O'-Lantern

Name _____

I'm going to make a jack-o'-lantern! Here is my pumpkin.

1

First, I make the eyes.

2

Next, I make a nose.

3

After the nose, I make a mouth.

4

Finally, I add a silly hat. Now I'm done!

5

Sequencing Practice Mini-Books, Grades K–1 © 2010 by Maria Fleming, Scholastic Teaching Resources

Let's Make Turkey Treats (pages 22–24)

Let's Make Turkey Treats

Name _____

Let's make a special turkey craft together. First, fold a piece of paper into a fan.

`1`

Next, glue the fan onto a paper cup. These are the turkey's feathers.

`2`

Then draw the turkey's face and wings. Cut them out.

`3`

Now glue the face and wings onto the cup. Then fill the cup with a yummy treat.

`4`

Finally, it's time to gobble, gobble up your treat!

`5`

Time to Brush! (pages 25–26)

Time to Brush!

Name _____

`1`

`2`

`3`

How to Make a Snowman (pages 27–28)

How to Make a Snowman

Name _____

`1`

`2`

`3`

A Gift for Bear (pages 29–31)

A Gift for Bear

Name _____

Look over there, under that tree. It's a gift! What can it be?

`1`

Take off the bow and paper, too.

`2`

It's a teddy bear for you!

`3`

Winter will not seem so cold with a teddy bear to hold.

`4`

Groundhog's Winter (pages 32–34)

Groundhog's Winter

Name _____

Before winter comes, groundhog eats lots of plants. He will not eat all winter long.

`1`

Now groundhog is nice and fat. He begins to dig a hole.

`2`

Groundhog digs a long tunnel with a small room at the end. This is called a burrow.

`3`

Groundhog sleeps in his burrow all winter. This long, deep sleep is called hibernation.

`4`

At last, winter is over. Groundhog leaves his burrow to stretch out in the warm sun.

`5`

A Penguin Grows Up (pages 35–37)

A Penguin Grows Up

Name _____

Peck, peck, peck!
A penguin chick hatches
from an egg.

1

After it hatches, the chick is
hungry. The penguin parents
feed it.

2

The chick eats and eats.
It grows fast. Now it has
fluffy gray feathers.

3

Then the chick loses its gray
fluff. It grows black and white
feathers like its parents.

4

At last, the penguin is all
grown up! It dives into the sea
with the other penguins.

5

A Valentine for Max (pages 38–40)

A Valentine for Max

Name _____

This is my cat, Max. I want
to make him a valentine.

1

First, I draw a big heart.

2

Next, I write his name
inside the heart.

3

Then I draw small hearts
around his name.

4

Finally, I give Max the
valentine. Max loves it!
And I love Max.

5

Growing a Garden (pages 41–42)

Growing a Garden

Name _____

1

2

3

Puddle Problem (pages 43–44)

Puddle Problem

Name _____

1

2

3

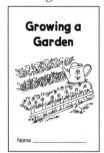

Becoming a Frog (pages 45–47)

Becoming a Frog

Name _____

This little tadpole is about
to go through big changes.

1

First, the tadpole grows legs.
Its tail gets shorter.

2

Next, the tadpole's eyes
and mouth grow bigger.
Its tail is almost gone now.

3

At last, the tadpole has
become a frog! It leaves
the water to live on land.

4

The Life of a Butterfly (pages 48–50)

The Life of a Butterfly

Name _____

Do you see the tiny dot on this leaf? It is a butterfly egg.

`1`

A caterpillar hatches from the egg. The caterpillar eats leaves and grows bigger.

`2`

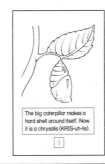

The big caterpillar makes a hard shell around itself. Now it is a chrysalis (KRIS-uh-lis).

`3`

Many days later, the chrysalis breaks open. The caterpillar has become a butterfly!

`4`

Five Little Raindrops (pages 51–53)

Five Little Raindrops

Name _____

Five little raindrops fell from the sky. The first one said, "Whee! I can fly!"

`1`

The second one said, "Ready, set, go!"

`2`

The third one said, "Look out below!"

`3`

The fourth one said, "Wait for me, everyone!"

`4`

The fifth one said, "Here comes the sun!" And that was the end of the raindrops' fun.

`5`

Get Ready for Baby Birds (pages 54–56)

Get Ready for Baby Birds

Name _____

Baby birds will be here soon! First, mama bird makes a nest.

`1`

Then she lays eggs in the nest.

`2`

Soon baby birds hatch from the eggs. Hello, little chicks!

`3`

Next, mama bird feeds the chicks worms.

`4`

At last, the chicks are big! They fly away. Bye, mama bird!

`5`

The Surprise Party (pages 57–59)

The Surprise Party

Name _____

Sheep came first with big balloons.

`1`

Pig came second with ice cream and spoons.

`2`

Hen came third with hats to wear.

`3`

Cow came fourth with cake to share.

`4`

Who came last? Farmer Fred! "HAPPY BIRTHDAY!" everybody said.

`5`

A Treat to Share (pages 60–61)

A Treat to Share

Name _____

`1`

`2`

`3`

Cool in the Pool (pages 62–63)

Cool in the Pool

Name _____

1

2

3

Hermit Crab's New House (pages 64–66)

Hermit Crab's New House

Name _____

I need a new house. My shell is too tight.

1

This sandcastle looks just right!

2

Oh no! Here comes a wave! It's very big! I must be brave!

3

Oh, well. My new home is gone. I will put my shell back on.

4

Ladybug and Bee (pages 67–69)

Ladybug and Bee

Name _____

Ladybug called her best friend, Bee. She said, "Please come play with me."

1

First, they hid among the flowers.

2

Next, they rode their bikes for hours.

3

Last, they see-sawed in the park.

4

They said goodbye when it got dark.

5

The Great Big Carrot (pages 70–72)

The Great Big Carrot

Name _____

One day, rabbit found a great big carrot. She pulled its leafy top.

1

"Let me help," said turtle. Turtle pulled rabbit. Rabbit pulled the carrot. But the carrot would not come up.

2

"Let me help," said mouse. Mouse pulled turtle. Turtle pulled rabbit. Rabbit pulled the carrot. But the carrot would not come up.

3

"Let me help," said an itty-bitty bug. She grabbed mouse's tail. Then the itty-bitty bug gave a great big tug.

4

POP! Up came the carrot! Then they all had a delicious carrot feast. And the itty-bitty bug ate the biggest piece!

5

Our Picnic Lunch (pages 73–75)

Our Picnic Lunch

Name _____

It's picnic time! What's inside our picnic basket?

1

First, we take out sandwiches.

2

Next, we take out apples.

3

After the apples, we take out grapes.

4

Finally, we take out cookies. What a yummy lunch to munch!

5